D0570017

ANNIE SLOAN

DECORATIVE

GILDING

ANNIE SLOAN

DECORATIVE

GILDING

A PRACTICAL GUIDE

Photography by Geoff Dann

Reader's Digest

THE READER'S DIGEST ASSOCIATION, INC

A Reader's Digest Book

Conceived, edited, and designed by
Collins & Brown Limited

Editor Colin Ziegler
Editorial Assistant Claire Waite
Art Director Roger Bristow
Designer Steve Wooster
DTP Designer Claire Graham
Photographer Geoff Dann

The acknowledgments that appear on page 96 are hereby made
a part of this copyright page.

Library of Congress Cataloging in Publication Data:

Sloan, Annie, 1949–
    Annie Sloan decorative gilding : a practical guide / Annie Sloan.
        p. cm.
    Includes index.
    ISBN 0-89577-879-3
    1. Gilding. 2. Bronzing. I. Title.
TT380.S59   1996
745.7'5–dc20   96-2746

Printed in Portugal

Contents

Introduction

L ONG CONSIDERED THE DOMAIN of the specialist, gilding is in fact far simpler and has a far wider range of applications than those tradition- ally associated with it. In *Decorative Gilding* we show how people with no previous knowledge of gilding can use a variety of techniques to revamp tired furniture, plain modern pieces, or even walls. We explain the whole process, from preparing the surface and applying metal leaf or bronze powders to adding further decoration and applying a final coat of varnish for protection. Each different technique contains step-by-step instructions; lists of tools and materials; countless ideas showing how to use the technique on furniture, small objects, and walls; variations and color combinations to try; and potential pitfalls to avoid.

Gilding on Glass

ABOVE To gild on glass (see pp. 30–33), you apply metal leaf either to part or the entire back of your object, then paint on top of this. When viewed from the front, the object exhibits a clear, perfect finish. Aluminum and Dutch metal leaf were laid on the back of this glass plate, with a little paint allowed to show through. You can use this technique to decorate interior windows, picture mounts, glass lights, and decorative glassware, such as bowls and goblets.

Hand Painting on Metal Leaf

ABOVE Here metal leaf – either Dutch metal, copper, or aluminum – is used as a background. Paint is applied on top, as a wash or as an opaque coat, with a lot of the background uncovered. This technique (see pp. 34–37) works particularly well on small items.

Paint Effects

ABOVE Paint effects (see pp. 38–41) create patterns over a background, and there are several different techniques worth trying. With metal leaf as the background over the entire surface, paint can be either dabbed with a rag (as above), sponge, or sheet of newspaper, or dragged with a brush or comb to create a textured effect.

The book is divided into two main sections: *Using Metal Leaf* (pp. 18–67) and *Using Bronze Powders* (pp. 68–87). Because they are cheaper than real gold or silver, Dutch metal leaf (imitating gold), aluminum leaf (imitating silver), and copper leaf appear most often in the techniques.

Metal leaf may be used on its own – in loose or transfer form (pp. 22–29) – on surfaces such as wood and plaster, or it may be used under glass. Other techniques combine metal leaf with paint, as in tortoiseshell (pp. 42–45) and incising (pp. 54–57), or with chemicals (pp. 62–67) to produce a distressed effect.

Beginners will want to start by using transfer metal leaf on a flat surface and then move on to loose metal leaf on a raised area. Applying loose leaf is tricky at first, because the leaf's lightness makes it difficult to control, but keep trying! Most techniques do not require perfect application, and the distressing technique actually works better when the leaf has wrinkles in it.

Gold Leaf

LEFT This candlestick was gilded with transfer real gold leaf. Although this is more expensive than imitation metals, it is not prohibitively expensive if you use it for small items. It has the advantage of not needing to be varnished, since it will not tarnish.

Tortoiseshell

ABOVE This exotic effect is achieved by applying transparent glazes and paint over Dutch metal leaf (see pp. 42–45). Traditionally used on small objects such as frames and boxes, tortoiseshell can be applied to larger items like the decorative shelf bracket shown here.

Highlighting Raised Surfaces

ABOVE Metal leaf looks highly effective on carved and molded objects, where the relief creates natural highlights and shadows. You can enhance this effect by painting over the gilded molding, then wiping the paint off the raised parts, so that it remains only in the recesses (see pp. 46–49).

Spirit Dyes

ABOVE These dyes look spectacular when applied over metal leaf, creating dramatic patterns and effects (see pp. 50–53). You can use them either neat or with denatured alcohol/methylated spirits. Whether you use brilliant colors (as above) or more restrained tones, you achieve an attractive, up-to-date result.

Aluminum Leaf

ABOVE On this mirror aluminum leaf, which does not tarnish, was used instead of the slightly more expensive silver leaf. Small squares of aluminum leaf have been cut out of a sheet of transfer metal leaf and positioned on the frame.

Bronze powders have a variety of uses as well. Traditionally they are applied over water- or oil-base size (pp. 72–75), either as a solid coat or sprinkled on top. You can also apply them in wax (pp. 80–83), either stenciled or rubbed on, or use them as a base for the verdigris technique (pp. 84–87). And you can create your own fun and inexpensive paint by adding bronze powder to varnish (pp. 76–79), a quick way to achieve a gilded effect.

The book concludes (pp. 88–91) with a number of examples that show how the techniques can be combined. Some of the projects that have already appeared in the book are shown again, with a second or third technique as an alternative.

To many people, gold and silver are associated with decoration in a grand, classical style. While this certainly provides one source of inspiration, it is not the only one. Look at the decorative traditions

Using Chemicals

ABOVE Most metal leaf tarnishes on contact with the air. You can increase this effect by using chemicals on the metal leaf (see pp. 62–67). Potassium sulfide with ammonia was used here over Dutch metal leaf.

Incising

ABOVE The beauty of incised paint lies in the contrast between the paint and the shiny metal leaf. To create this effect you paint over a coat of metal leaf, then reveal some of the leaf again by drawing with a soft but firm implement into the wet paint (see pp. 54–57).

Distressing

ABOVE This technique (see pp. 58–61) re-creates the look of old furniture on which metal leaf has rubbed off over the years to reveal the basecoat below. These painted chair legs were covered in metal leaf and then distressed with steelwool. This breaks up the leaf into tiny pieces, leaving traces of metal on the painted surface. Distressing works best on furniture or frames.

Bronze Powders

LEFT These fine, metallic powders come in various colors, including golds, coppers, and silver (see pp. 70–75). Here bronze powders were sprinkled over a molding that was first colored and sized.

of India, China, and South America for other ways in which gold and silver can be used. These styles depart from restrained European colors to introduce strong, bright colors that can be used to create a contemporary look. Their designs offer many varied motifs, such as spots, stars, and crescents. Look at fabrics and jewelry for ideas; and consider illuminated manuscripts, early church paintings, and decorated china from all over the world when you are searching for design ideas.

Using gold, silver, and copper in a room creates brightness, sparkle, and a focus for the eye. More importantly, it gives light. Put any metallic object in the dark corner of a room and the reflective quality of the metallic finishes makes the whole area come alive.

Approach all the techniques in this book with a spirit of adventure and experimentation, and you will get the most out of the fascinating art of decorative gilding.

Metallic Paints

ABOVE By mixing bronze powders with either varnish or a fabric paint medium you can make a versatile paint that is fun and easy to use (see pp. 76–79). Then transform plain fabrics, walls, and furniture easily and cheaply into stunning works of art.

Metallic Wax

ABOVE You can use metallic waxes (see pp. 80–83), either homemade or bought from an art supply store, to make patterns and lines, stencil walls or furniture, touch up the edge of a frame, or create a light, textured look. The easiest way to apply metallic wax is with your finger, adding a mere hint of gold. Here gold wax was stenciled over a brown base.

Verdigris

ABOVE This technique (see pp. 84–87) imitates the aging of real copper that has been exposed to the air. A green paint and denatured alcohol/methylated spirits mix is dripped over a base of copper-colored metallic wax and shellac. Generally applied to small objects, verdigris is used here on a plaster gargoyle shelf bracket.

Preparing Surfaces

*Putty knife
for applying
filler*

*Ready-
made filler*

*Sanding
block and
sandpaper*

Soft cloth

*Paint and
water*

*Soft brush
for apply-
ing paint*

Rust inhibitor

*Small and large
brushes for removing
and applying paint
remover*

*Wire brush
for rubbing
off loose
rust*

*Paint
remover*

BECAUSE ANY IMPERFECTIONS in a surface are very noticeable under metal leaf, gilding is usually done on a smooth surface. Even brushmarks from the painted base can show up. In order to obtain a really good finish, you should fill wood (whether new or old) with a fine filler and then rub it down, repeating the process until the surface is completely flat. New metal will be smooth enough, but old metal needs preparing so that it is even and unlikely to rust.

Preparing Wood

1 Apply a small amount of ready-made filler at a time with a putty knife. Press down hard to smooth the filler and fill up dents in the wood. Allow to dry.

2 Using a sanding block wrapped in a piece of medium-grade sandpaper, rub all over the surface, first with the grain, then against it.

3 Add 1 part water to 9 parts paint, stir well, then apply to your entire surface, using a good soft brush. Smooth it out thoroughly and allow it to dry.

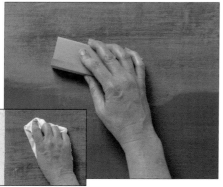

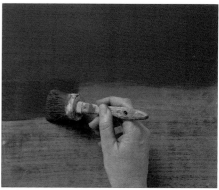

4 Rub the surface down with fine sand-paper over a sanding block and wipe it clean with a cloth (inset). If necessary repeat steps 1, 2, 3, and 4.

5 Paint the surface again, this time using undiluted paint. Spread the paint out well to create a thin coat with no brushmarks showing.

Preparing Rusty Metal

1 Rub the metal hard, using a wire brush to remove all loose and powdery fragments of rust.

2 Paint the surface with rust inhibitor, carefully following the instructions for the brand you are using.

3 Allow to dry. The old metal should now have lost its rusty appearance and have a smooth surface.

4 Paint your object all over with a paint specifically designed for use on metal.

Repairing a Picture Frame

1 Using a small bristle brush, apply a generous amount of paint remover to the frame. Leave until the paint softens or bubbles.

2 Wash the frame with water and use a firm bristle brush to remove all loose pieces, especially from the crevices.

3 Apply another coat of paint remover, making sure you reach all areas of the frame. Leave to soften again, then remove as before.

4 With a piece of paper towel, wipe off any excess water and any remaining flakes of paint. The surface of the frame is now clean of years of dirt and successive layers of paint that obscured the carving.

5 Mix 2-part molding clay according to the instructions (inset) and apply a small piece to any broken areas, smoothing it down with a dampened finger until it is the correct shape (above). Leave to dry for 24 hours.

Gold Size

To apply either metal leaf or bronze powders you need a special glue called gold size, which does not tarnish the metals. Both water-base and oil-base size are available. Water-base size is the easiest for the beginner. You use it to coat a surface, and after 15 minutes you can apply leaf or powder to it. It remains tacky indefinitely, so there is no hurry to complete your work. However, since it never dries, you can only use it if you cover the whole of your sized area with powder or leaf. Otherwise, you must use oil-base size; for this you need to wait until it has the tackiness of adhesive tape, which can take between 10 minutes and several hours. It remains tacky for only a short time and then dries and becomes unworkable.

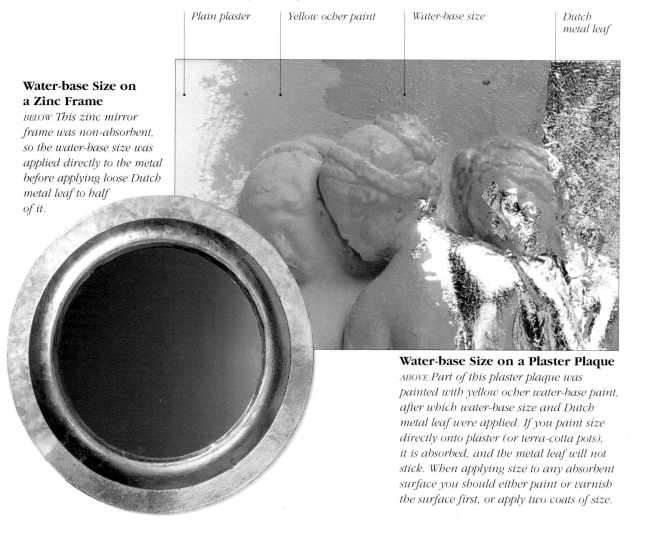

Plain plaster   Yellow ocher paint   Water-base size   Dutch metal leaf

Water-base Size on a Zinc Frame

BELOW This zinc mirror frame was non-absorbent, so the water-base size was applied directly to the metal before applying loose Dutch metal leaf to half of it.

Water-base Size on a Plaster Plaque

ABOVE Part of this plaster plaque was painted with yellow ocher water-base paint, after which water-base size and Dutch metal leaf were applied. If you paint size directly onto plaster (or terra-cotta pots), it is absorbed, and the metal leaf will not stick. When applying size to any absorbent surface you should either paint or varnish the surface first, or apply two coats of size.

Sizes on Paints of Different Absorbency

LEFT On this board, the different paints were applied in horizontal strips and the different sizes in vertical strips. Note how both sizes considerably darken the color of the absorbent paint and how oil-base size has a much shinier finish than water-base size.

Oil-base size over non-absorbent paint

Oil-base size over absorbent paint

Water-base size over non-absorbent paint

Water-base size over absorbent paint

Bowl of oil-base size and a soft, flat brush for applying it

Bowl of water-base size and a soft, flat brush for applying it

Water-base Size over Bamboo and Wood

RIGHT Because real bamboo (right) is non-absorbent, water-base size was applied directly to this piece. The new wooden molding (below right) had to be painted first, since new wood absorbs size.

Water-base size

Dutch metal leaf

Plain unpainted wood

Terra-cotta paint

Water-base size

Aluminum leaf

Varnishes

YOU NEED TO VARNISH all bronze powders and metal leaf to prevent them from tarnishing. The only exceptions are real gold leaf and, to a certain extent, aluminum leaf, which does not tarnish but dulls over time. A coat of varnish is also useful if you are using certain techniques on top of metal leaf, such as hand painting on metal leaf (pp. 34–37), paint effects (pp. 38–41), tortoiseshell (pp. 42–45), highlighting raised surfaces (pp. 46–49), and incising (pp. 54–57). The varnish protects the leaf so that you can wipe off mistakes and start again without marking or tearing the leaf.

THE COLOR OF VARNISHES

When you apply water-base varnish to metal leaf, it at first appears white, but dries completely clear within 15 minutes. When you apply shellac to metal leaf, a white opaque bloom appears after 5–10 minutes, but it too soon disappears.

Water-base varnish   *Shellac*

Immediately after application

After 5–10 minutes

After 15 minutes

Varnished using oil-base varnish

Unvarnished

Oil-base varnish with soft brush for applying it.

The Effect of Oil-base Varnish

ABOVE *The left hand side of this panel was coated with oil-base varnish, making it darker and glossier than the right hand side. The panel's border was first covered with Dutch metal leaf, which was decorated with a mix of blue and yellow spirit dyes. In the central panel bronze powders were applied in a line and in a pattern over water-base size. The urn relief was done in Dutch metal leaf with spirit dyes on certain areas.*

Two traditional varnishes have stood the test of time: oil-base varnish and shellac. Oil-base varnish (sometimes called polyurethane) is very strong but takes about 6 hours to dry. You can use it to protect all metals, spirit dyes, and bronze powders. Shellac (sometimes called French polish) dries within 5 minutes but is not as strong. It comes in many shades of brown. Both varnishes have a yellowish tinge that barely shows over copper, gold, and Dutch metal leaf, but is obvious over silver and aluminum. A more modern varnish, water-base varnish (sometimes called acrylic varnish), has not yet had time to prove its durability. No one knows whether it will tarnish the metal leaf underneath. Water-base varnish dries within 10–15 minutes, is strong, and can be used over all surfaces except spirit dyes and bronze powders over water-base size.

Using Varnish with Chemicals

BELOW This candlestick was covered in loose copper leaf. Then bleach was applied in places, to make greenish-blue patches. The finish was left to oxidize for two days, then coated with oil-base varnish to halt the process.

Varnished using shellac

Unvarnished

Shellac with a soft, flat brush for applying it.

The Effect of Shellac

ABOVE The lightest shellac was applied over the left hand side of this panel. The base was first covered with metal leaf and waxed – as was the central raised motif. The shellac gives light protection, and acts as a base for other techniques. For stronger protection, apply oil-base varnish over the shellac.

Colors and Metallic Finishes

W HEN CHOOSING YOUR colors consider both what colors will work well next to your metallic finish and what colors will look good showing through the finish. Metallic finishes have a certain sophistication, so they tend to need muted colors. You can use bright primary colors, but they need the right context. Gold leaf is traditionally used over a terra-cotta base, but deep reds and browns similarly look very effective. Copper generally needs cooler colors – greens, blues, and grays – to provide a contrast to its warm orange or pink tones, while the white and gray tones of silver, aluminum, and pewter work well with all colors.

Take care not to use colors that are too deep with metal leaf, or they will appear black against the bright reflective quality of the leaf. Metallic waxes are not as shiny, so they can take a darker tone. That considered, do not be afraid to try whatever color combination appeals.

Blue and Dutch metal leaf

Deep red and gold bronze powder

Dark green and gold metallic wax

White and Dutch metal leaf

Brown and gold bronze powder

Terra-cotta and gold bronze powder

Black and copper leaf

Medium blue and copper bronze powder

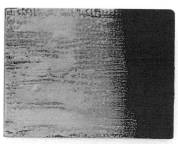

Strong blue and copper metallic wax

Brown and copper leaf

Bright green and deep copper bronze powder

Gray and copper metallic wax

Deep red and aluminum leaf

Deep blue and silver bronze powders

Purple and pewter metallic wax

Black and aluminum leaf

Gray and silver bronze powders

Cool brown and pewter metallic wax

Using Metal Leaf

Tools and Materials

Loose Metal Leaf

BELOW These less expensive types of metal leaf are the most commonly used in decorative gilding. They can be applied to all surfaces but must be handled with care, as they tear easily.

METAL LEAF CAN BE USED TO decorate walls, furniture, and smaller objects such as frames and vases. Available in both loose and transfer leaf (leaf that has been pressed onto waxed tissue paper for easier handling), metal leaf is applied to a surface with size, then smoothed down with special gilding brushes. You may find silver and gold leaf too expensive for your purpose. If so imitation gold leaf (usually known as Dutch metal or brass leaf), imitation silver leaf (made from aluminum), and copper leaf provide a less costly alternative.

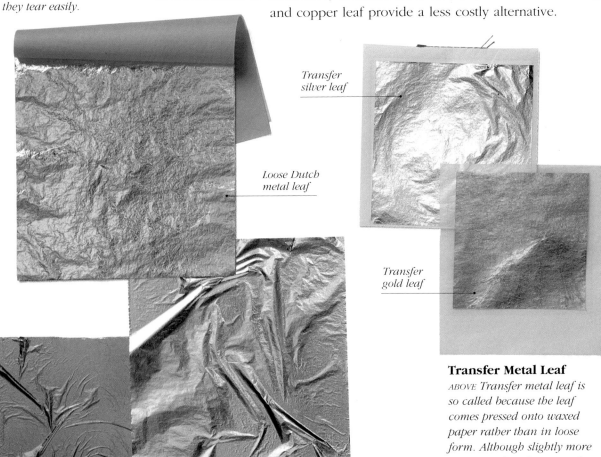

Transfer silver leaf

Loose Dutch metal leaf

Transfer gold leaf

Loose aluminum leaf

Loose copper leaf

Transfer Metal Leaf

ABOVE Transfer metal leaf is so called because the leaf comes pressed onto waxed paper rather than in loose form. Although slightly more expensive than loose metal leaf, transfer leaf is easier to handle and can be cut into decorative shapes with scissors (right). Dutch metal, copper, and aluminum can also be bought in transfer form.

Oil-base size

Water-base size

French Chalk

ABOVE To prevent metal leaf – and especially loose metal leaf – from sticking to your fingers and tearing, you need to cover your hands with French chalk. Talcum powder may be used as a substitute.

Water-base Size & Oil-base Size

LEFT AND ABOVE Size, also called gold size, is a special-ized glue used to adhere all types of metal leaf. Water-base size remains tacky indefinitely while oil-base size dries completely, becom-ing clear (see pp. 12–13).

Ox-hair brush for applying size to larger areas

Small brush for drawing intricate designs in size

Brush for applying size

Gilder's tamper

Gilder's mop

Scissors for cutting transfer leaf

Gilding Brushes & Brushes for Applying Size

LEFT These gilding brushes are used for pushing down the leaf smoothly without tearing it. The gilder's mop is used for smoothing large flat areas, while the gilder's tamper is good for pushing loose leaf into small awkward areas on carved surfaces. Choose high quality brushes for applying size so that the size will cover evenly without leaving any brushmarks.

Loose Metal Leaf

A NY METAL LEAF – copper, aluminum, silver, gold or Dutch metal – that comes without a sheet of waxed paper backing is called loose leaf. Because loose leaf is very light, it crinkles and tears easily, making it harder to apply than transfer leaf (see pp. 26–29); even a draft can affect the laying of the leaf. We do not demonstrate the use of loose real gold leaf in this book, because it is too difficult for the novice gilder to handle. Despite these concerns people often prefer loose leaf to transfer leaf, because it costs less and works well on carved surfaces (which transfer leaf does not), and for the distressing technique (see pp. 58–61).

Gilded Chair

This chair was painted off-white, with very dark brown paint applied in the recesses. Loose Dutch metal leaf was then applied, allowing the background paint to show through at the top of the chair and on the legs. The metal leaf was covered with an oil-base varnish.

TOOLS & MATERIALS

The Basic Technique

Paint

Brush for applying paint

Water-base size and brushes for applying it

Gilder's tamper

Gilder's mop or soft brush for dabbing metal leaf

French chalk or talc for dusting fingers

Sheet of loose metal leaf

1 Paint your surface (see p. 10). Allow to dry. You can use either water- or oil-base paint, flat or glossy, although oil-base paints can take up to two weeks to dry.

2 Apply a coat of size. Water-base size is best for the beginner, since it remains tacky indefinitely giving you more time to complete your work.

3 To prevent the metal leaf from sticking to your fingers, dust them lightly with French chalk or talc before handling it.

4 Take a sheet of loose metal leaf in both hands and lower it carefully into position, starting at one edge and easing the rest into place. If a sheet tears, try to match up the edges as closely as possible.

5 Using a gilder's mop or a soft brush, smooth the metal leaf onto the surface. Dab it down, rather than wiping it, so that it does not tear before adhering properly.

6 Continue to cover the surface, slightly overlapping sheets of metal leaf. Wipe away any excess leaf with the gilder's mop, saving excess to fill gaps (see p. 24).

Filling Gaps

  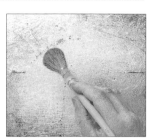

1 To fill gaps, holes and tears in the surface, pick up a small excess piece of metal leaf, using a gilder's mop or a finger dusted in French chalk.

2 Press the piece into the gap, using your fingertip or the gilder's mop. If it does not stick, add more size to the exposed surface and reapply the metal leaf.

3 When all the gaps are filled, gently brush away any excess metal leaf. Brushing too briskly will break the metal leaf into pieces too tiny to use.

PITFALLS
Brushmarks, grit, or hair from a brush all show up under loose metal leaf. Begin with a smooth, dust-free surface and use good, soft brushes.

Applying Loose Metal Leaf in Selected Areas

1 Paint a design on your surface, either freehand or using a stencil, with any water- or oil-base size (see pp. 12–13). Allow it to dry.

2 Tear pieces of metal leaf off the sheet and dab them onto the design, pressing down all over to make sure they have stuck.

3 Wipe away all excess metal leaf. Using a soft brush, rub firmly over the entire design to make certain that the leaf is adhering.

Distinctive Vase
ABOVE *Irregular rectangles were painted in water-base size over the surface of this blue china vase. The rectangles were then overlaid in a varied pattern of loose copper, aluminum, and Dutch metal leaf.*

Applying Loose Metal Leaf to a Carved Surface

1 *Using a small brush to reach the intricate areas, apply a coat of water-base size, making sure the whole surface is covered. Allow to dry.*

2 *Tear the metal leaf into small enough pieces to cover the surface in sections. Don't use a whole sheet or the metal leaf will break.*

3 *When the size is tacky dab the leaf pieces gently onto the surface with your fingers, pushing them into position around the carving.*

4 *Rub the surface with your fingers to bring out the carving's details. Use a gilder's tamper for more intricate areas.*

5 *To cover up any holes, push excess metal leaf into position with the gilder's tamper.*

6 *Brush off excess metal leaf and fill in any remaining gaps. You can now color the surface, distress it, or simply leave it as it is. Because aluminum leaf was used here, the surface does not need varnishing (see pp. 14–15).*

Transfer Metal Leaf

Checkered Frame

A blue papier-mâché frame was coated with oil-base size, and cut-out squares of transfer aluminum leaf were positioned around it. The hard end of a brush was used to scribble on each square, making a slightly indented pattern.

ALL METAL LEAF CAN BE bought in the form of transfer leaf, which is lightly attached to waxed paper. The backing makes handling the metal leaf easier, because the paper strengthens the leaf and slightly overhangs it, giving you something to hold. Beginners should start with transfer leaf, especially when a smooth, even metal coat is desired. If using real gold, always use transfer gold leaf; loose gold leaf requires specialist equipment. Transfer leaf is the best choice for making decorative geometric shapes, because it can easily be cut with scissors. By cutting the precise amount to fit an object, you can avoid wastage.

TOOLS & MATERIALS

Soft pencil (artist's 3B) for drawing lines

Pair of sharp scissors

Metal ruler

Sheet of transfer metal leaf

French chalk or talc for dusting fingers (optional)

Transfer metal tape

Oil-base size

Water-base size and soft, flat brush for applying size

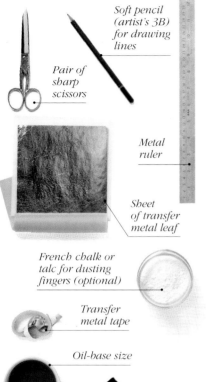

The Basic Technique

1 After sizing the surface (see p. 23), position the transfer leaf, holding it by the overhanging waxed paper. Slightly overlap edges of additional sheets. Work carefully; once the leaf is applied, it cannot be moved.

2 Place the leaf in position, then smooth the paper with your fingers, particularly at the edges. The waxed paper will come loose as the transfer leaf sticks to the size.

3 Using a soft brush, wipe excess leaf from the overlapping sheets. If there are any gaps, try to reapply a piece of transfer leaf, using more pressure. If this does not work, add more size and then reapply the leaf (see Filling Gaps p. 24).

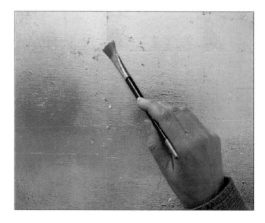

Making Lines Using Transfer Metal Tape

1 In pencil, mark the position for your transfer metal tape. Use a soft pencil so that the line remains clear even after you have added the size.

2 Paint oil-base size, which becomes clear when dry, over the line with a soft, flat brush. Cover an area broader than the transfer tape.

3 When the size is tacky and your hands chalked, apply the tape to the surface as shown in The Basic Technique *above*.

Cutting Decorative Shapes

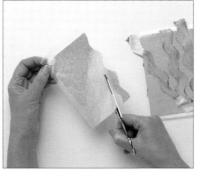

1 *Draw your design on the paper side of the transfer leaf. Try simple, bold patterns at first; complicated designs may cause the leaf to work loose from the paper.*

2 *Using very sharp scissors, cut out the shapes, holding onto the overlapping waxed paper edge as you do so. Open the scissors wide each time to make certain of a good, clean cut.*

3 *After covering your surface with oil-base size, which becomes clear when dry, place each shape in position, carefully smoothing over it with your fingers to secure it.*

4 *Remove the waxed paper (inset), which should come free naturally if the transfer leaf has adhered properly. You can create a variety of shapes (above), as long as they are not too complex.*

Green and Gold Mirror

ABOVE *The frame of this oval mirror has been painted green, then stripes and diamonds of transfer Dutch metal leaf have been applied, interspersed with a few small squares. The frame was protected with oil-base varnish.*

Applying Transfer Gold Leaf

1 Real gold leaf is very thin and needs a smooth surface. Paint the surface, rub it down with wet-and-dry fine sandpaper; paint and sand it again, then paint it one more time.

2 Apply the water-base size evenly with a soft brush, being careful not to apply it so thickly that brush-marks show. Allow it to set for 10–15 minutes.

Real Gold Frame

BELOW An unpainted oak frame was gilded with real gold, which reveals the grain of the wood. Real gold leaf does not need varnishing, as it does not tarnish with time.

3 Real gold transfer leaf comes in smaller sheets than the other metal transfer leaf, but you apply it in the same way (see The Basic Technique *on p. 27).*

Gilded Lamp Base

ABOVE The thinnest available real gold transfer leaf was used on this wooden lamp base. It has broken up slightly in places, where it was bent around the base, giving glimpses of the terra-cotta paint beneath.

Gilding on Glass

Gilded Cabinet Doors
The four small diamond shapes on the doors of this glass cabinet were gilded with loose Dutch metal leaf, using water-base size. A coat of bright blue paint on the back of the gilded glass creates a vivid contrast to the metal leaf.

GILDED GLASS EFFECTS ARE achieved by applying metal leaf to the underside of an object. You then view the finished work through the glass. Whether you apply the metal leaf to part of the object or cover it completely, the effect is particularly pleasing, because the metal leaf appears even and perfect through the glass. To protect the metal leaf and prevent it tarnishing, you may either use oil- or water-base varnish (see pp. 14–15) if the whole glass area is gilded or, for partly gilded glass, coat the back with paint, which enhances the metal color and gives definition to the design. Aluminum does not need protection, so you may use it without painting or varnishing.

METAL LEAF ON GLASS IN CLOSE-UP

The tree shapes were first painted in water-base size. Size quickly becomes transparent on glass, so it helps to attach an exact drawing to the other side of the glass to act as a guide throughout the process.

TOOLS & MATERIALS

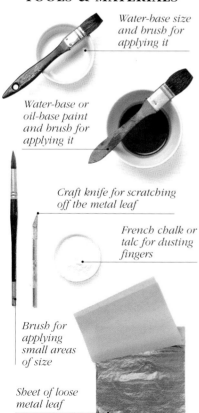

Water-base size and brush for applying it

Water-base or oil-base paint and brush for applying it

Craft knife for scratching off the metal leaf

French chalk or talc for dusting fingers

Brush for applying small areas of size

Sheet of loose metal leaf

The Basic Technique

1 Using a soft brush, coat the back of the glass thinly with water-base size. Leave to dry for about 10–15 minutes, or until it is tacky.

2 Dust your fingers with French chalk, then prepare some loose metal leaf by tearing it into small pieces of different shapes and sizes.

3 Gradually build up your pattern by placing pieces of the torn metal leaf on the tacky glass. Put some pieces close together and others farther apart. Rub them lightly to stick them securely to the glass and to make the metal leaf even and smooth.

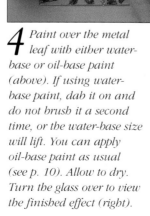

4 Paint over the metal leaf with either water-base or oil-base paint (above). If using water-base paint, dab it on and do not brush it a second time, or the water-base size will lift. You can apply oil-base paint as usual (see p. 10). Allow to dry. Turn the glass over to view the finished effect (right).

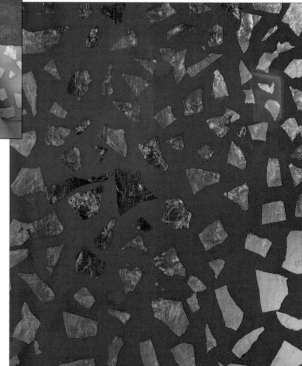

Incising Metal Leaf on Glass

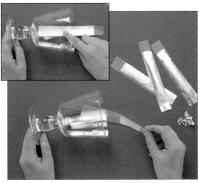

1 *Paint evenly-spaced stripes of water-base size inside a goblet and leave to dry. When it becomes transparent, you can turn the glass in the light against a dark background to see where you have worked.*

2 *Cut transfer metal leaf – here aluminum – into strips for easier handling. Place a strip over each stripe of size in the goblet (inset), then rub the backing paper with your finger until the leaf works loose (above).*

3 *Using a soft brush, rub the surface of the metal leaf to remove all the excess particles. You should end up with clean, sharp stripes of metal leaf.*

4 *With a craft knife, incise designs – here, swirls, loops, dots, and lines – by scratching into the leaf. You do not need to protect aluminum leaf, but the finished product is strictly decorative. Washing it would remove the leaf, because you used water-base size.*

PITFALLS

Choose background colors with care. Here, a rich green looks almost black in contrast to the metal leaf, when seen through the glass and size. Select a paint that is slightly brighter than the color you want.

Gilded Plate

BELOW *Circles of transfer Dutch metal leaf were applied at random to this glass plate and most of the rest of the surface was gilded with aluminum leaf. A back coat of bright green protects the design and allows a little color to show through.*

Incised Bowl

LEFT The basic leaf shapes and band were painted onto the inside of this Pyrex bowl with water-base size. Transfer aluminum leaf was then applied, and geometric designs scratched into it.

COLOR COMBINATIONS

Dutch metal on deep red and pink

Latticework Mount

RIGHT A gilded latticework mesh was created on a glass mount with loose Dutch metal leaf. Some areas were rubbed to remove a bit of the leaf, creating a textured look. The surface was protected with water-base varnish.

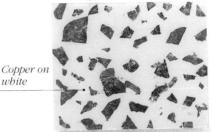

Aluminum and some Dutch metal on medium green

Copper on white

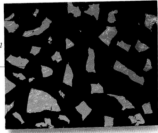

Aluminum on black

Gilded Bowl

LEFT This Pyrex bowl was coated with water-base size, and covered randomly with loose aluminum, copper, and Dutch metal leaf. The bowl was lightly washed so that the leaf came off in places. When dry, the inside was painted bright red.

Hand Painting on Metal Leaf

Decorated Door

Drawing inspiration from Indian and Ancient Egyptian decoration, this door was painted with an off-white flat paint. Loose Dutch metal leaf was applied to the panels; then the potted plant designs, dots, and lines were added, using water-color paint.

T HE PROCESS OF HAND PAINTING on metal leaf is an ancient one. Using shiny metal leaf as a background gives the paintwork a jewel-like quality that is decorative and bright. As the metal leaf catches the light it appears to glow in contrast to the paint. Water-base paints, which are flat, provide a complete contrast to the glossy metal leaf. The natural sheen of oil-base paints works well when the paint is applied either thinly as a wash or densely. You can dilute either the water-base or the oil-base paints to allow the metal leaf to show through a translucent veil of color. For inspiration look at early illuminated manuscripts from Ancient Egypt, at medieval paintings, or at works from China, Japan, the Middle East, and India.

TOOLS & MATERIALS

Water-base paint
(this may be
decorator's paint),
Gouache, or
watercolor

Small brush
for applying
paint

Preparing the Surface

*Due to the waxy surface of
metal leaf it can be difficult
to get paint to adhere to the
surface (right). To prevent
beading, add a drop of
dishwashing liquid (you
may need more if you are
using transfer leaf backed
with waxed paper) to your
water-base paint (inset).
Or you can coat your metal
leaf first with shellac or
oil-base varnish (see pp.
14–15). This also allows you
to wipe off any mistakes
more easily.*

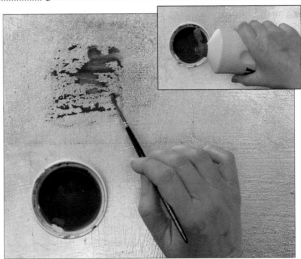

The Basic Technique

1 *After applying loose
or transfer metal leaf
(see pp. 23 and 27),
create your design plan.
It is possible to wipe the
paint off immediately
after you have applied it,
but if you do this too
often the metal leaf
begins to wear away.*

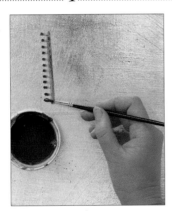

2 *A highly-diluted
paint creates cloudy
veils of color. You may
need to add more dish-
washing liquid to very
watery paint. Do not add
too much however, or
bubbles will appear.*

3 *Use less diluted paint to make a variety of marks
against the gold background. When you use water-
base paint the colors can become lighter or duller over
time. To retain strong, clear colors, protect the surface with
a coat of varnish (see pp. 14–15) when it is dry.*

Using Artist's Oil Paints

You can easily apply artist's oil paint over metal leaf (above) without the addition of any de-greasing agent such as dishwashing liquid. Unlike water-base paint, oil-base paint retains its color and finish after drying (right).

Gold and Black Candlestick

ABOVE *This was gilded with loose Dutch metal leaf, then covered with oil-base varnish. The designs were painted with black oil-base paint.*

Printing Paint on Metal Leaf

LEFT *As a quick alternative to painting, you can coat corrugated board with paint and use it to print on the leaf.*

Hand-Painted Plant Container

LEFT Transfer aluminum leaf was applied to the surface of this small plant container, then painted with oil-base paint. In places the silver color shines through the thinned green paint, giving the container a slightly luminous quality.

Hand-Painted Box

RIGHT The red base was gilded with loose Dutch metal leaf to cover the lid and form a band resembling a landscape on the sides. Clumps of grass, flowers, and trees on the base, and stylized clouds on the top were added with water-base paint.

Hand-Painted Chair Back

LEFT AND BELOW Loose Dutch metal leaf was applied over this wooden chair back, and the scene was painted with water-base paints. The indented areas were painted black to resemble bamboo stems.

COLOR COMBINATIONS

Green and blue on copper

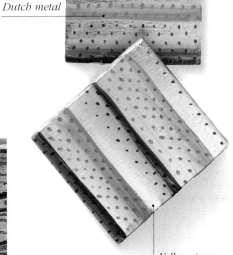

Green and blue on Dutch metal

Yellow, terracotta, and crimson on Dutch metal

Yellow, terracotta, and crimson on aluminum

Paint Effects

Frottaged Pot

*This clay pot was sealed
with water-base varnish,
then covered with loose
Dutch metal leaf. The top
band was frottaged using
yellowish-green paint, the
alternate stripes using
terra-cotta that echoes the
pot's natural color.*

P AINT EFFECTS ARE TECHNIQUES that make patterns – sometimes random,
sometimes exact – over a background, usually of paint but here of metal
leaf. One of the simplest techniques, *frottage*, entails blotting thinned,
water-base paint from a surface with newspaper. Other techniques, such as
sponging, ragging, dragging, and combing, use a combination of glazing medium (see p. 40) and paint to make a translucent colored glaze, over which a
tool is drawn to reveal the metal leaf beneath. Depending on the colors used,
paint effects can give an exotic and rich, or antique and distressed look. You
can also use them as a background for freehand painting.

Despite the coat of water-base varnish, the size was absorbed into the clay in places, preventing the metal leaf from sticking properly all over. This gives the pot added texture and pattern.

TOOLS & MATERIALS

Thinned water-base paint

Brush for applying paint

Crumpled newspaper

The Basic Technique

1 *After applying loose or transfer metal leaf (see pp. 23 and 27), paint over it with a thinned water-base paint (approximately 2 parts paint to 1 part water). If the paint does not adhere properly, add some dishwashing liquid (see p. 35).*

2 *Crumple a sheet of newspaper (above) and then spread it over the painted surface while the paint is still wet. Smooth the paper out with your hands to absorb the paint (right).*

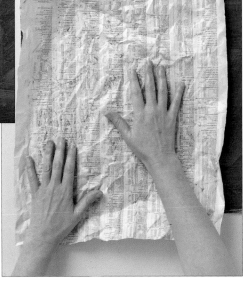

3 *Carefully peel the newspaper away from the surface. The result should be a random pattern, with the metal leaf shining through in places and covered by paint in others.*

ALTERNATIVES

For many paint effects you need to add transparent glazing medium to your paint to make it translucent and to keep it wet longer. Glazing medium, which is available in art supply stores, should be used in a proportion of 1 part glaze to 4 parts paint. Here, the mixture was brushed on, then dabbed with a rag (right) and sponge (far right).

Dabbed with a rag

Dabbed with a sponge

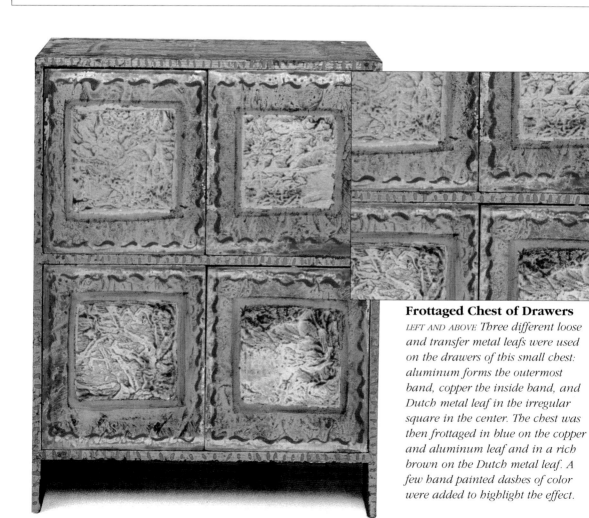

Frottaged Chest of Drawers

LEFT AND ABOVE Three different loose and transfer metal leafs were used on the drawers of this small chest: aluminum forms the outermost band, copper the inside band, and Dutch metal leaf in the irregular square in the center. The chest was then frottaged in blue on the copper and aluminum leaf and in a rich brown on the Dutch metal leaf. A few hand painted dashes of color were added to highlight the effect.

Marbled Clock

RIGHT The marble effect on this clock was created by frottaging in terra-cotta on aluminum leaf. The warm paint over the whitish metal leaf results in a cool-ish pink color.

COLOR COMBINATIONS

Blue on Dutch metal

Terra-cotta on Dutch metal

Greenish-grey on aluminum

Pale blue on Dutch metal

Paint Effect Samples

RIGHT AND BELOW Both these effects have been created using glazing medium (see p. 40) and water-base paint. The blue sample (right) has been combed, while the brown sample (below) has been dragged with a dry brush.

Tortoiseshell

Tortoiseshell Box

This wooden box was first covered with loose Dutch metal leaf. It was then tortoiseshelled, using an oil-base glazing medium mixed with dark brown pigment and tinged with a little reddish-brown. The gold color of the base gives considerable depth to the box.

THIS GLAZING TECHNIQUE IMITATES natural tortoiseshell markings, which are translucent in some places and opaque in others. Over Dutch metal leaf, this technique gives the depth and the slightly see-through look you need. Both real and imitation tortoiseshell have been popular since the shell was first imported to Europe in the 17th century. The technique works best on flat or smoothly rounded surfaces – on other surfaces the badger-hair softening brush tends to remove the glaze and paint instead of blending it. To authentically imitate the platelets of the tortoiseshell, create small sections in your pattern. Also remember that you cannot carve or bend real tortoiseshell very much. You may, of course, create tortoiseshell fantasies of your own, varying the color, size, and intensity of the markings.

TOOLS & MATERIALS

The Basic Technique

Liquid dryers

"Boiled linseed oil" and brush for applying paint

Raw sienna oil-base paint

Burnt umber oil-base paint

Brushes for applying glaze

Badger-hair softening brush

Water-base glazing medium

Burnt sienna pigment

Burnt umber pigment

1 Make an oil-base glaze by mixing 3 parts "boiled linseed oil" to 2 parts liquid dryers. Stir them together thoroughly.

2 After applying loose Dutch metal leaf to the surface (see p. 23), cover it with a coat of the glaze, using diagonal strokes.

3 Dab on different-size patches of raw sienna oil-base paint with a soft-bristle brush dampened with turpentine. Do it thinly, using diagonal strokes.

4 Apply burnt umber oil-base paint in the same way. Paint it on in patches, covering some areas heavily and leaving others free of paint.

5 Use the tip of a badger-hair softening brush to blend the colors over the glaze. Brush first in the original direction of the marks, then in the crosswise direction, to achieve a soft look without brushmarks.

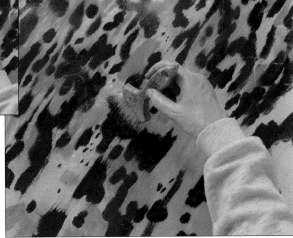

6 You can enhance the tortoiseshell effect by adding small areas of dry, burnt umber paint with a blunt-ended brush (above). Then soften them in all directions using a badger-hair brush (right).

Using Pigments

Instead of artist's oil paints and oil-base glaze, you can use pigments and water-base glazing medium to imitate the look of tortoiseshell. Pigments and glazing medium are available in most good art supply stores.

1 After applying loose Dutch metal leaf to the surface (see p. 23), cover it with a coat of water-base glazing medium (see p. 40), using diagonal strokes.

2 Mix burnt sienna and burnt umber pigments into some more glazing medium. In each mix, use about 1 part pigment to 10 parts glaze.

3 Using a soft, round brush paint a variety of marks in burnt umber, stroking mainly in the same direction. Add a tiny amount of burnt sienna.

4 Blend the colors as in Step 5 of The Basic Technique (see p. 43). You can give extra depth by adding more burnt umber glaze, creating darker areas that lie on top of the blended colors.

5 Soften the colors again with the badger-hair brush (above), so that they blend without leaving brushmarks. The end result (right) should be a mixture of shapes and sizes.

Tortoiseshell Obelisk

ABOVE On this obelisk, burnt sienna and burnt umber artist's oil paints and oil-base glaze were used over loose Dutch metal leaf. The base and middle molding were left as unpainted metal leaf.

COLOR COMBINATIONS

Raw sienna and burnt umber on Dutch metal

Raw Sienna and Burnt Umber Bracket

LEFT This plaster bracket was first painted a deep brownish-red. Then the inner panels, top, and edging were overlaid with loose Dutch metal leaf. Applying raw sienna and burnt umber artist's oil paints to an oil-base glaze allowed the brownish-red to add definition and contrast.

Viridian and burnt umber on Dutch metal

Crimson and Burnt Umber Frame

RIGHT AND BELOW This old frame was tortoise-shelled in the previously plain concave area. Alizarin crimson and burnt umber artist's oil paints were applied over loose Dutch metal leaf.

Burnt umber on Dutch metal

PITFALLS

Using too much paint here has obliterated the golden base and blurred too much in the soften-ing process. The tortoiseshell effect would be enhanced by adding more dark brown and decreasing the burnt sienna, applied in less regular shapes with better balance of contrast.

Alizarin crimson and burnt umber on Dutch metal

Highlighting Raised Surfaces

Highlighted Plant Trough

The terra-cotta plant trough was covered first with Dutch metal leaf, then with white paint, which was wiped off the raised parts. The relief is rather rough, so a little white paint remains in the design.

G ILDING CREATES A dramatic effect on carved or molded surfaces, where the light casts shadows and gives shape to the molding. The surface is first covered with loose metal leaf (see p. 25), and paint is applied to the gilded surface. When the wet paint is wiped off the raised parts, the metal leaf shows through and is caught by the light. A dark-colored paint provides the greatest contrast against the metal leaf; a pale color creates a more delicate look. If you rub too hard at the wet paint, a little of the metal leaf may lift off. This technique works best with a soft paint such as poster paint or gouache, since it is easier to wipe off.

TOOLS & MATERIALS

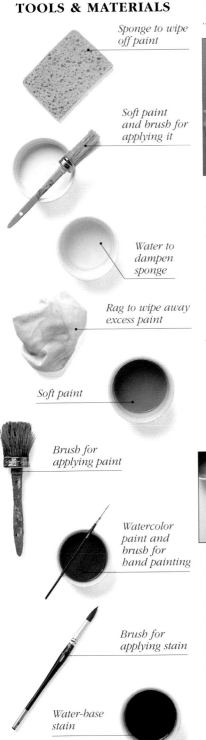

Sponge to wipe off paint

Soft paint and brush for applying it

Water to dampen sponge

Rag to wipe away excess paint

Soft paint

Brush for applying paint

Watercolor paint and brush for hand painting

Brush for applying stain

Water-base stain

The Basic Technique

1 After covering your raised surface with loose metal leaf (see p. 25), brush paint – here, white – over the entire area.

2 Dab firmly over the surface with the brush. Make sure that no leaf shows through, and that no puddles of paint form in the depressions.

3 Using a lightly damp-ened sponge, gently wipe the wet paint from the raised part of the surface. Do not rub too vigorously or you will break the surface of the leaf, revealing the base color.

Gilding on Raised Wallpaper

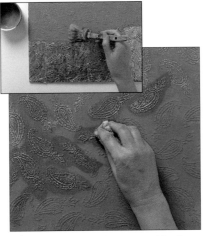
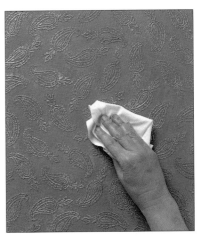

1 After applying loose metal leaf (see pp. 23 and 25), apply a soft, flat, paint (inset). Allow to dry. Wipe the uppermost surface gently with a small, damp sponge.

2 With a dry cloth wipe away any traces of wet paint that remain on the pattern. The raised pattern should look shiny against the paint.

Hand Painting on Wallpaper

1 *After gilding your wallpaper, or frieze (see p. 25), carefully paint the background, which is not raised. Use a fine brush and watercolor paint, adding enough water to make the paint translucent rather than opaque. Allow to dry.*

2 *To enhance and define its three-dimensional quality, apply a dark water-base woodstain to the edges and crevices of the raised areas.*

Gilded Chair

LEFT AND BELOW The raised relief panels on the back of this 1930's chair were gilded in Dutch metal leaf, and black paint was used to define the design.

Highlighted Mirror

ABOVE The aluminum leaf base was covered with dark blue paint. The still-wet paint was wiped off on the raised areas as shown in The Basic Technique (see p. 47).

Gilded Plaque

RIGHT The plaster plaque was covered in Dutch metal leaf, then painted a greenish-blue. To provide a strong contrast, more paint was wiped off in some areas than others.

PITFALLS

Metal leaf sometimes has a waxy surface that water-base paints have difficulty adhering to. To avoid this add a drop of dishwashing liquid to the paint and mix well. Do not use too much or bubbles form in the paint. If you prefer not to expose traces of base color, you can prevent any metal leaf from lifting by protecting it with a coat of oil-base varnish (see pp. 14–15).

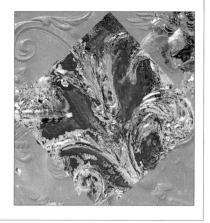

COLOR COMBINATIONS

Bright blue on Dutch metal

Pale blue-green on copper

Raised Wallpaper

RIGHT Dutch metal leaf and red paint were applied over this raised wallpaper. The paint was wiped away from the raised areas with a soft sponge and dry cloth. The background was then painted again with a deep red, thinned down to give it a translucent quality.

Reddish-brown on Dutch metal

Black on aluminum

Spirit Dyes

S PIRIT DYES PROVIDE a dramatic way of coloring metal leaf. Although they are called "dyes," they actually lie on the surface of the leaf without dying or staining it. Translucent and with the consistency of ink, they come in intense colors, which are very strong if undiluted – a little goes a long way. When you drip or draw denatured alcohol/methylated spirits onto a layer of spirit dye, you reveal the metal leaf while creating a ring or line of darker color around the edge. First, experiment with colors individually over different metal leafs, and with denatured alcohol/methylated spirits, to learn to control the dyes and make patterns and shapes. Protect the finished effect using an oil-base varnish (see pp. 14–15).

Dyed Cabinet

All surfaces of this small cabinet were gilded with loose Dutch metal leaf. The vase shape was then painted in black spirit dye and decorated by dropping denatured alcohol/methylated spirits to suggest contours on the base. The stems and flower shapes were created using some neat and some diluted spirit dye. The blue background was added last, along with the informal pattern of stripes and spots that decorate the rest of the cabinet.

The Basic Technique

1 After gilding your surface with loose or transfer metal leaf (see pp. 23 and 27), use a soft brush to coat it with spirit dye. Apply dye and paint sparingly on a horizontal surface, or the dye will drip down.

2 Using a soft pointed brush, either drop some denatured alcohol/methylated spirits onto the spirit dye or touch the surface with the brush. The latter allows more control over the positioning.

3 Soak the brush again in denatured alcohol/methylated spirits and drag it along the surface to make lines. Wait a little after each brushstroke to see the full effect. You can add more denatured alcohol/methylated spirits if the effect is not dramatic enough.

TOOLS & MATERIALS

Concentrated spirit dye

Soft brush for painting on spirit dye

Denatured alcohol/ methylated spirits and soft pointed brush for applying it

4 Drying takes only a few minutes and will reveal areas that still need work (right). When the first layer is dry, you can go back over some areas a second or third time (above).

Achieving other effects

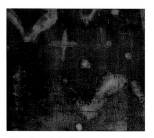

Loose Dutch metal leaf was coated in red artist's oil paint. Then mineral spirit/turpentine (a thinner of oil-base paint) was dropped onto it to create an organic pattern.

Black spirit dye was painted over loose aluminum leaf, then spotted with denatured alcohol/methylated spirits to make designs. The process was then repeated with blue spirit dye.

Loose Dutch metal leaf was streaked twice with orange, red, and brown spirit dye. In successive applications denatured alcohol/methylated spirits was poured down it, then splattered over it.

Patches of yellow, orange, and green spirit dyes were painted on dutch metal leaf. Then much of the surface was darkened with black spirit dye, leaving small areas of bright color.

PITFALLS

The coat of spirit dye should be thin and translucent. If you apply it too thickly, you will not be able to see the metal leaf underneath. Even after you add denatured alcohol/methylated spirits, the spirit dye will remain opaque. In this event wipe it off and start again, using a very thin coat.

Tartan Letter Rack

RIGHT Lines of blue and orange spirit dyes were painted over loose copper leaf. Thicker lines of blue spirit dye were then drawn with a brush filled with denatured alcohol/ methylated spirits, which caused them to spread.

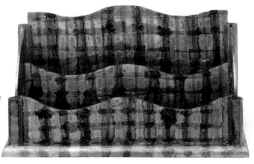

Dyed Frame

RIGHT This frame was overlaid in loose aluminum leaf then coated in a mixture of black and brown spirit dye. Lines were made at intervals around the frame using a brush soaked in denatured alcohol/ methylated spirits, so the dyes would run.

Mottled Box

BELOW AND RIGHT This box was covered with random scraps of loose aluminum, copper, and Dutch metal leaf. Brown and red spirit dyes, with a little blue added, were painted over these, then spotted with denatured alcohol/methylated spirits to create a rich effect like a polished stone.

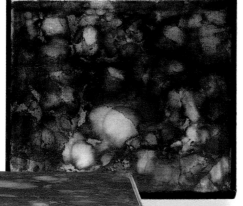

COLOR COMBINATIONS

Blue on copper

Yellow on Dutch metal

Black and brown on aluminum

Red on Dutch metal

USING SHELLAC

If you apply shellac (see pp. 14–15) over transfer Dutch metal leaf and leave it for 20 minutes to dry but not harden, you can then paint the surface with spirit dye and use denatured alcohol/methylated spirits to soften the shellac in places, creating swirls and even making areas of shellac peel off.

Shellac and brush for applying it

Black, blue, and brown spirit dyes

Swirls

Areas of shellac peeled off

Incising

T HE INCISING TECHNIQUE INVOLVES applying metal leaf to a surface and then painting over it. You remove the paint by drawing into it while it is still wet, to reveal the shiny metal leaf underneath. Incising has long been used decoratively and can be seen on many old frames, but lends itself to both classical and modern designs. Flat-finish paint acts especially well as a contrast to the shiny metal. You can use any object to draw into the paint. Make sure the incising tool is soft enough not to break the metal leaf but firm enough to be controlled.

Incised Chest of Drawers

The drawers of this modern pine chest were gilded with Dutch metal transfer leaf, then painted off-white. Marks were then made in the paint, using a sliver of cork, that revealed the leaf below. The rest of the chest was painted a pale blue, then brushed drily with a coat of off-white paint. In places, such as just under the drawer knob (below), both paint and Dutch metal leaf were removed to reveal the warm color of the pine base.

TOOLS & MATERIALS

The Basic Technique

Cotton swabs

Half a cork

Plastic comb cut in half

Brush for applying paint and varnish

Mounting putty (Blu-Tack)

Small piece of poster board

Water-base paint

Water-base varnish

Slightly blunt craft knife

Small screwdriver

1 Apply loose or transfer metal leaf (see pp. 23 and 27) and protect it (top) with varnish (see pp. 14–15). Cover the dry surface with water-base paint (above).

2 You can use any firm material with a soft edge to wipe away the still-wet paint. Cotton swabs work well but absorb paint quickly, so have several ready.

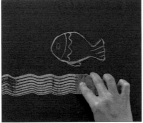

3 Use a small plastic comb to make a wavy effect or make a similar comb out of stiff poster board.

4 Use a piece of mounting putty (Blu-Tack) for making dots. Knead it often since it absorbs paint.

5 A sliver of cork makes a clear, clean line. Regularly remove excess paint from the cork.

6 To make a more textured mark that does not remove the paint so cleanly, use either a piece of poster board (above) or a cork cut in half (right). Experiment with other materials too.

Incising Through Metal Leaf

The process of incising through paint to reveal the metal leaf below can be reversed to create an attractive alternative. In this technique a layer of metal leaf is incised to reveal the paint underneath. Because a topcoat of metal leaf makes this technique costly, it is most suitable for small items.

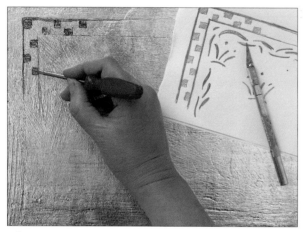

1 *Cut down on mistakes by first sketching out your design on paper and using this as a guide. Make your design by scratching away parts of the metal leaf with a small screwdriver.*

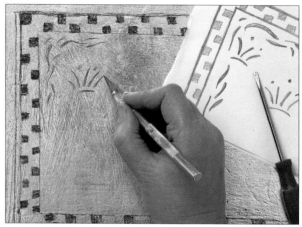

2 *Use a slightly blunt craft knife to incise fine lines. If working on wood, be sure the surface is well painted, or it will be difficult to draw across the grain of the wood.*

PITFALLS

When scratching through paint, take care not to scratch too hard, or you may remove the metal leaf, revealing the base surface. Varnishing the leaf helps to prevent this. Or you can try using oil-base size rather than water-base size.

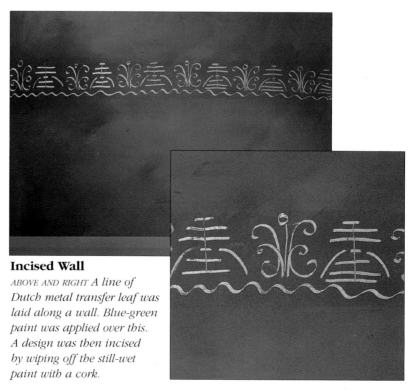

Incised Wall

ABOVE AND RIGHT A line of Dutch metal transfer leaf was laid along a wall. Blue-green paint was applied over this. A design was then incised by wiping off the still-wet paint with a cork.

Dotted Frame

RIGHT AND BELOW This wooden frame was gilded in copper transfer leaf, then painted a deep reddish-crimson. While it was still wet, small dots were made in the paint using a piece of mounting putty (Blu-Tack).

COLOR COMBINATIONS

Terra-cotta on Dutch metal

White on Dutch metal

Bright blue on copper

Blue-black on aluminum

Incised Cupboard

LEFT This small cupboard was gilded in loose aluminum leaf, then painted a rich blue. The tree drawing was incised through still-wet paint with cotton swabs.

Incised Houses

RIGHT This design of houses and a tree was incised through deep gray-blue wet paint laid over Dutch metal transfer leaf. The drawing was created using the handle end of a paintbrush for a thin, delicate line for greater detail.

Distressing

O NE OF THE DELIGHTS OF old gilded objects is the way the metal leaf has worn away in places to show the color underneath. You can re-create this look in your own gilding by rubbing wax – either good quality furniture wax or beeswax – gently over the metal leaf with very soft steelwool. This breaks the leaf up into tiny pieces, leaving traces of metal on the painted surface. The technique does not have to look traditional; for a more contemporary look use brightly colored backgrounds, or rub through the metal leaf to make shapes. A coarser steelwool dipped in either turpentine or water will create a more pronounced effect – a good technique for large objects.

Distressed Cupboard

The emerald green base was coated with oil-base size. Sheets of transfer copper leaf were applied with spaces in between, making a diamond lattice pattern. The surface was then distressed with medium-gauge steelwool dipped in turpentine and protected with oil-base varnish.

DISTRESSING IN CLOSE-UP

Applying the metal leaf with accuracy is difficult. Once the leaf has stuck, you cannot move or reposition it, so you need to make a virtue of any fault that you have created. Scratch away at areas where the gaps are too large or too small.

TOOLS & MATERIALS

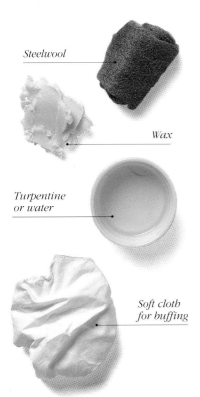

Steelwool

Wax

Turpentine or water

Soft cloth for buffing

The Basic Technique

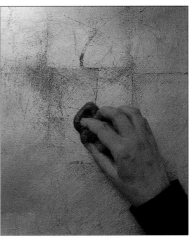

1 After painting the surface and covering it with loose or transfer metal leaf (see pp. 23 and 27), rub over it with very fine steelwool dipped in wax. Use clear or colored wax.

2 Using a non-waxy part of the steelwool, rub over the leaf to remove parts of it. Any areas of the leaf that have folded or crinkled will produce a more obvious mark.

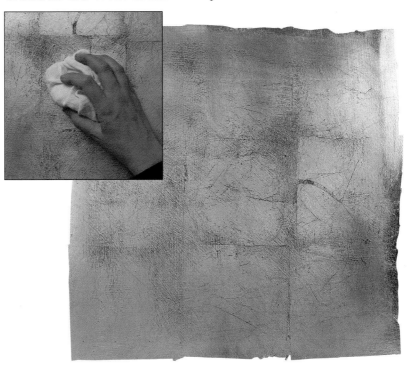

3 Leave the wax to harden for about 10 minutes, then buff to a soft sheen (inset). The wax initially dulls the metal leaf, but when buffed gives it a soft, mellow shine like old gold (above).

Making a Pattern in the Leaf

1 Make patterns by rubbing hard in certain areas to reveal the color underneath. Here fine steelwool dipped in clear wax was rubbed in lines over aluminum leaf.

2 After finishing the design, rub wax all over until you cannot see any areas of unwaxed leaf. Leave to harden for 10 minutes.

3 Buff the entire surface of the patterned and waxed leaf with a soft cloth (above) to give an overall sheen (below).

ALTERNATIVE

You can combine two different colors of metal leaf, using one on top of the other. Here, Dutch metal leaf was laid over a terra-cotta surface, then an aluminum layer was applied randomly on top, leaving some gaps. The whole effect was then rubbed back with soft steelwool to show glimpses of both the Dutch metal and even the terra-cotta base.

Distressed Drawers

BELOW *These drawers were covered with several bright colors and overlaid with transfer Dutch metal leaf. The surface was rubbed back to create flower patterns and then buffed.*

Highlighted Frame

ABOVE Dutch metal leaf was laid over the terra-cotta base of this frame. It was rubbed back with fine steelwool and dark wax, removing some areas almost completely and leaving others shiny gold. The surface was then buffed.

COLOR COMBINATIONS

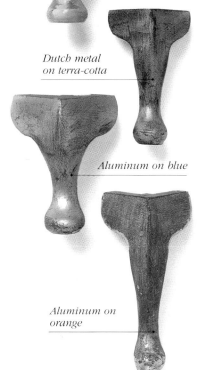

Copper on greenish-blue

Dutch metal on white

Dutch metal on terra-cotta

Aluminum on blue

Aluminum on orange

Distressed Bureau

ABOVE This dark blue desk was overlaid with loose aluminum leaf, rubbed with wax using steelwool, then buffed. Where the leaf tore, more of the blue can be seen.

Antiqued Candlestick

ABOVE This candlestick has a terra-cotta base color, with Dutch metal leaf on top. To achieve the effect of an old, worn object, clear wax and the finest steelwool were used to rub away some of the metal leaf. The surface was then buffed.

PITFALLS

If paint or size is not applied evenly and with care, brush-marks may be left on the surface that will become more apparent when the metal leaf is rubbed with steelwool and wax. This detracts from the paint-and-metal leaf effect.

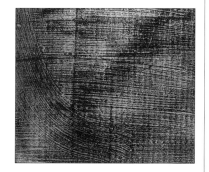

Using Chemicals

T HERE ARE MANY DIFFERENT chemicals that you can apply to metal leaf, either to discolor it or to eat through it to reveal patches of the color underneath. Sodium sulfide, potassium sulfide, and cupric nitrate are all effective and available from specialist art supply stores; common household products such as bleach or ammonia also work. The effects vary according to the chemicals, their strengths, and the type of metal leaf that you use, so experiment first on a small piece of leaf before tackling a whole surface. When you are happy with the effect, you can stop the reaction by washing off the chemicals with water or by varnishing the surface.

Silvered Writing Box
This old, gray-blue painted box was first gilded with loose aluminum leaf. Bleach was then dripped onto it, blackening the metal leaf and in places eating it away completely to reveal the color beneath. Finally, the surface was varnished with shellac to give it an even sheen.

TOOLS & MATERIALS

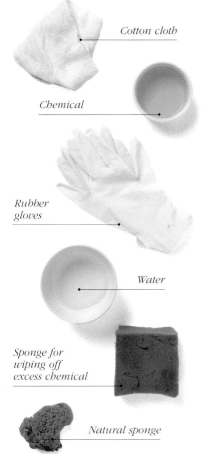

Cotton cloth

Chemical

Rubber gloves

Water

Sponge for wiping off excess chemical

Natural sponge

Applying Chemicals

1 With goggles and rubber gloves for protection, roll the corner of a cotton cloth into a point and dip it in the chemical, here copper patinating fluid.

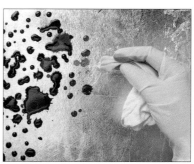

2 Drip the fluid onto the surface of the metal leaf in small and large drops, with more in some areas than in others to give variety.

3 When you have achieved the desired effect – the effect works more quickly on Dutch metal and copper leaf than on aluminum and silver – wipe off the excess patinating fluid with a sponge. This will also spread the chemical in a diluted form to give a delicate patination.

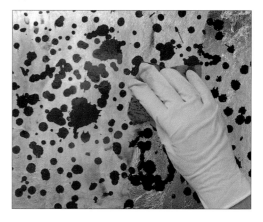

Sponging on Chemicals

1 Protecting your hands with rubber gloves, dip a small piece of natural sponge into diluted patinating fluid (3 parts fluid to 1 part water) and dab it onto the metal leaf.

2 Wipe off the excess fluid with a separate wet sponge to give a delicate, dappled effect. To vary the look dab on a few drops of water in places to dilute the fluid further.

3 Leave the fluid on the surface for 1–5 minutes, depending on how pronounced an effect you want, and then wash it all off.

Making Streaks with Chemicals

1 *Soak a rag in patinating fluid and apply it generously along the edge of the metal leaf.*

3 *Once you have the desired effect in one direction, you can repeat the process in the opposite direction to give a random, checkered pattern. Varnishing the surface with shellac (below) reduces the verdigris patination (right).*

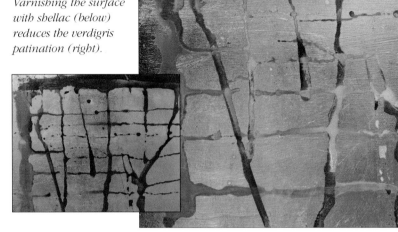

2 *Tilt your surface so that the edge with the fluid is highest and the fluid runs across the surface.*

Drawing with Chemicals

You can create patterns on metal leaf by dipping the twisted corner of a piece of cloth into a chemical and using it as a drawing implement (above). Use a small amount of patinating fluid first to see how strong the reaction is. If the result is not bold enough, strengthen the design by going over it again with more fluid (right).

Experimenting with Chemicals

Copper is the easiest metal leaf to patinate. Dutch metal, which contains copper, reacts more slowly, while aluminum is affected only very little.

When mixing a chemical with diluted ammonia, you should keep on adding the chemical until no more of it will dissolve in the diluted ammonia.

4 parts potassium sulfide to 1 part ammonium sulfate on Dutch metal leaf over terra-cotta

2 parts potassium chloride to 1 part sodium chloride on copper leaf over terra-cotta

Hydrochloric acid (spirits of salt or descaler) on copper leaf over green

Copper carbonate in diluted ammonia (1 part ammonia to 1 part water) on copper leaf over terra-cotta

Ferrous sulfate on copper leaf over terra-cotta

Hydrochloric acid (spirits of salt or descaler) on aluminum leaf over green

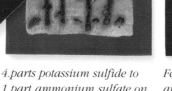

Copper carbonate in diluted ammonia (1 part ammonia to 1 part water) on Dutch metal leaf over terra-cotta

4 parts potassium sulfide to 1 part ammonium sulfate on copper leaf over terra-cotta

Ferrous chloride in diluted ammonia (1 part ammonia to 1 part water) on Dutch metal leaf over terra-cotta

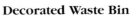

Decorated Waste Bin

ABOVE Transfer copper leaf was applied over this waste basket, then a saturated solution of sodium sulfide used to draw the designs. Around the dark lines of the drawing, multicolors resembling oil spills can be seen (varnishing will remove these).

Gilded Clock

ABOVE Loose Dutch metal, copper, and aluminum leaf were all used to decorate this pendulum clock, then discolored with chemicals in places.

Copper Leaf Tray

RIGHT Strong chemicals have eaten away the loose copper leaf on this tray to reveal a bright orange-red base. The tray was covered with shellac and oil-base varnish to make it usable.

Two Candlesticks

RIGHT AND BELOW The one on the right was covered with loose copper leaf, then marked in areas with potassium sulfide. To produce the bluish patches on the one below, copper nitrate was dribbled on Dutch metal.

Dutch Metal Candle Holder

ABOVE The loose Dutch metal leaf on this candle holder was discolored in a design with patinating fluid; in places the process revealed the base color underneath.

COLOR COMBINATIONS

Dutch metal on blue

Copper on terra-cotta

Silver on terra-cotta

Dutch metal on terra-cotta

PITFALLS

By using a solution that is too strong, or by leaving it on the metal leaf for too long, you can turn the leaf completely black. Sometimes the base color shows through, which can provide an interesting contrast. Experiment with different strengths of chemicals and different lengths of time.

Using Bronze Powders

Tools and Materials
Bronze Powders
Metallic Paints
Metallic Wax
Verdigris
Combining Techniques

Tools and Materials

RONZE POWDERS ARE very fine powders that come in a range of metallic colors. Despite their name, they are not in fact made of bronze. The "silver" powder is actually aluminum, while the rest are varying mixtures of copper and zinc. Traditionally they are used over oil-base size, either in a solid pattern or sprinkled on top to create a glittery varnish. You can also use them in wax, to stencil or to add finishing touches with a thin gold line. By adding the powders to varnish, you can create paints for fabrics, walls, or furniture. Bronze powders produce less shine than metal leaf, but they are generally easier and cheaper to use.

Rich pale gold

Pale gold

Orange gold

Antique copper

Crimson copper

Light gold

Medium gold

Deep copper

Copper

Fire copper

Bronze Powders

ABOVE AND RIGHT *Bronze powders are available in a wide range of colors, including several golds, from light yellow modern golds to dark golds and older, reddish golds. There are also several copper colors, ranging from modern to old coppers and the more spectacular crimsons.*

Silver

Greenish-gold

Reddish-gold

Pewter

Silver

Medium gold

Copper

Metallic Waxes

LEFT *Several colors of ready-made metallic waxes are available from art supply stores. For other colors you can mix your own by combining clear wax with a bronze powder.*

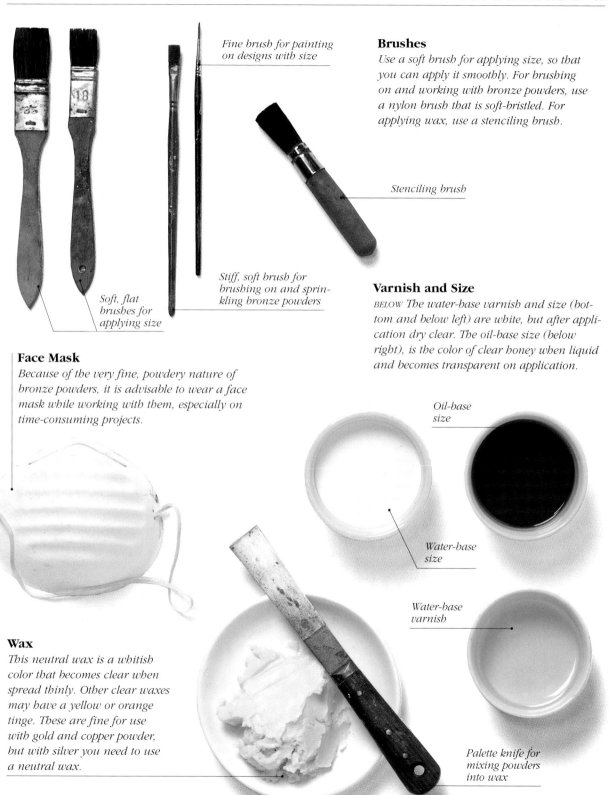

Fine brush for painting on designs with size

Brushes

Use a soft brush for applying size, so that you can apply it smoothly. For brushing on and working with bronze powders, use a nylon brush that is soft-bristled. For applying wax, use a stenciling brush.

Stenciling brush

Soft, flat brushes for applying size

Stiff, soft brush for brushing on and sprinkling bronze powders

Varnish and Size

BELOW *The water-base varnish and size (bottom and below left) are white, but after application dry clear. The oil-base size (below right), is the color of clear honey when liquid and becomes transparent on application.*

Face Mask

Because of the very fine, powdery nature of bronze powders, it is advisable to wear a face mask while working with them, especially on time-consuming projects.

Oil-base size

Water-base size

Water-base varnish

Wax

This neutral wax is a whitish color that becomes clear when spread thinly. Other clear waxes may have a yellow or orange tinge. These are fine for use with gold and copper powder, but with silver you need to use a neutral wax.

Palette knife for mixing powders into wax

Bronze Powders

Bronzed Curtain Finial

The design on this finial was painted in water-base size, and different-colored bronze powders were then brushed on in various places. Stars and parallel lines were also painted in size on the wall and bronze powders brushed on. When working on a vertical surface, brush on a little powder at a time and work from top to bottom.

AFTER METAL LEAF, BRONZE POWDERS create the shiniest and most metal-lic effect. Traditionally you use bronze powders by dusting the fine particles onto gold size so that they adhere. You can also sprinkle the powder over a tacky coat of oil-base size or brush it onto a stenciled or hand painted design. Do this technique in a draft-free environment, because bronze powders are extremely fine and liable to blow around. You should also wear a face mask for protection against breathing in dusty particles. The size will not tarnish the metals, but you should coat your finished work with oil-base varnish for a long-lasting effect. Early American settlers used bronze powders with stencils, often placing designs of fruit and flowers in gold on a dark-colored background. Your own design does not have to be compli-cated – a simple arrangement of spots and dots can be highly effective.

TOOLS & MATERIALS

Dark gold bronze powder

Copper bronze powder

Medium gold bronze powder

Small bristle brush for dusting on bronze powder

Water-base size and fine brush for applying it

Large, soft bristle brush for removing loose bronze particles

Face mask for breathing safely

Brush for applying oil-base size

Oil-base size

Soft pencil (artist's 3B)

The Basic Technique

1 Paint the surface evenly with a coat of oil-base size. Oil-base size (see pp. 12–13) will dry and become clear on the parts of the surface that are not covered by the bronze powders.

2 When the surface is tacky, pick up a little bronze powder on a small bristle brush and tap the brush gently to make the powder fall onto the surface.

3 A second, third, or even fourth bronze powder may be added to give the effect more life. For a different look, apply powders while the oil-base size is wet rather than tacky. This causes the powders to spread slightly. Or you can dust the powders solidly in some areas to give variation.

Painting a Design with Bronze Powders

1 Stencil or trace your design in pencil, if you wish, then paint it on with size. Since you will cover the whole design area with bronze powders you can use water-base size. Its longlasting tackiness allows you plenty of time to complete your work.

2 When the size has dried to tacky, take a small amount of bronze powder on a bristle brush. Brush the powder onto the drawing, pushing it ahead of the brush. This minimizes the chance of smudging the sized line, in case it is still wet.

3 You can add an extra element to your design by using two or more different-colored bronze powders. Leave areas of your design unpowdered and fill them in, as in step 2, using different-colored bronze powders.

4 When you have finished applying the bronze powders, dust away any loose powder particles with a soft bristle brush to reveal the design. Any excess powder can be collected and used again.

ALTERNATIVE

If you sprinkle a little water over oil-base size, it acts as a barrier between the size and the powder. When you sprinkle bronze powders over the wetted surface, the powders only adhere in areas where the size is not covered with water. Here (right) the process was done twice resulting in a chance arrangement of dark green, warm gold and cool gold.

Sprinkling Bronze Powders

These two pieces of molding were painted – deep red (top) and green (bottom) – covered with oil-base size, and then sprinkled with different-colored bronze powders as marked.

| Warm gold | Silver | Medium gold | Crimson copper |

| Light gold | Warm gold | Silver |

Star-like Tray

LEFT The star-like effect comes from sprinkling silver powder over a dark blue base coated with oil-base size. The rim was brushed with copper powder and the whole tray was protected with oil-base varnish.

COLOR COMBINATIONS

Pale gold on dark pink

Silver on grey

Reddish-copper on white

Medium gold on dark green

Striped Frame

RIGHT This frame, which was originally plain green, was painted with strips of oil-base size. Then a yellowish-green gold bronze powder was sprinkled on these areas. The surface was protected with oil-base varnish.

PITFALLS

If the size is wet, rather than tacky, when you dust away the loose particles the powder spreads (see tail). If the size is put on too thickly, it creates a thick raised line of bronze powder (see clump of grass).

Bronzed Box

ABOVE Whimsical designs were painted on in water-base size and covered with different-colored bronze powders. The surface was protected with oil-base varnish.

Metallic Paints

Decorative Plant Pot

This terra-cotta pot was first painted all over in bright blue. A simple design was then applied with gold metallic paint, using a small brush.

METALLIC PAINTS ARE FUN and easy to use, although they lack the brightness and intensity of metal leaf or bronze powders. Many different types are available ready-made from art supply stores, but you can easily make your own by adding bronze powders to an oil-, water-, or denatured alcohol/methylated spirit-base medium. Oil-base paints need shaking frequently – the powders tend to sink to the bottom – but they have the advantage of preserving the luster of metallic colors and preventing them from tarnishing with age. For large quantities, use a water-base varnish with bronze powders – it is inexpensive and readily available.

METALLIC PAINT IN CLOSE-UP

The design used here was taken from a china saucer. The simple gold patterns that decorate fine porcelain can provide a great source of inspiration.

TOOLS & MATERIALS

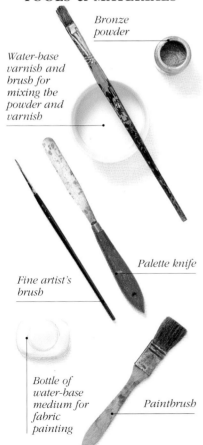

Bronze powder

Water-base varnish and brush for mixing the powder and varnish

Fine artist's brush

Palette knife

Bottle of water-base medium for fabric painting

Paintbrush

Making Metallic Paint

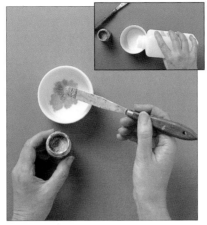

1 Pour some satin or gloss water-base varnish into a container (inset). Add enough bronze powder, using a spoon or palette knife, to make an opaque but still runny paint.

2 Mix the paint with a brush until it is completely blended. Do not make more than you need, as it tends to dry out quickly, even in an airtight container.

Applying Metallic Paint

1 Use a paintbrush to cover large areas such as a wall or piece of furniture. If you miss an area, allow the paint to dry completely before retouching.

2 For small designs, use a fine artist's brush and add a little water to help the paint flow. Clean your brush frequently, or it will become clogged with dried paint.

Making Metallic Fabric Paint

1 *In a container, combine a special fabric paint medium, available at art supply stores, with the bronze powder. Adjust the amount you use according to your fabric and the thickness of paint you require.*

2 *Mix thoroughly with a brush. Mix only a small amount at a time, as it tends to dry out quickly.*

Spotted Fabrics

RIGHT A fine purple cotton is painted with silver color spots. Spots and rings have been applied to the sheer, bright green fabric, using a crimson copper and medium gold color. On the heavier pink cotton, copper and pale gold have been used.

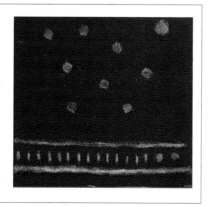

3 *Apply the paint to the fabric with a brush or sponge (left), taking care not to create any lumps. Allow to dry, then cover with a cotton cloth and press with a medium to hot iron (above) to set.*

PITFALLS

Fabric paint does not adhere well to coarse fabrics or to those with a thick pile, such as velvet (right). By using a sponge you can get enough paint to stick, but this may result in a thick, crusty layer of paint on the surface.

Stenciled Fabric

RIGHT This gold and copper design was stenciled onto the brown hessian with a sponge.

COLOR COMBINATIONS

Silver on white

Copper on pale blue

Striped Wall

ABOVE This white wall was painted with stripes of gold metallic paint. Between the stripes a gold leaf motif was stenciled. Gold paint was then applied to corrugated cardboard and pressed against the white panels, leaving uneven lines. White was pressed onto the gold panels.

Classical Candelabra

RIGHT This design, based loosely on 19th-century glass lights, was painted in a medium warm gold over a rich maroon basecoat.

Medium gold on unpainted terra-cotta

Gold and Green Curtain Pole

LEFT This wooden curtain pole was first painted a dark gold. The gold was then enhanced with traditional designs in a dark green water-base paint.

Green-gold on olive-green

Metallic Wax

Metallic-waxed Chest of Drawers

The black base was rubbed all over with a greenish-gold metallic wax, using a finger to give the streaked appearance. A copper-colored wax was used to create the stenciled designs on each drawer.

METALLIC WAX MADE OF CLEAR WAX combined with bronze powders, is the easiest to use of all the gilding materials. It can be bought ready-mixed from art supply stores, but is also easy to make yourself. You can apply it with your finger, adding it to the tips of carvings or the edges of frames to give just a hint of gold. You can also use it to stencil patterns and lines. Metallic wax is not as bright and shiny as metal leaf or even bronze powders, but it allows ease and speed of use, and creates softer, mellower tones. Although the wax hardens on drying, coat it with shellac then oil-base varnish for full protection (see pp. 14–15).

Making Metallic Wax

1 Take some clear wax and add approximately the same amount of bronze powder. Don't worry if you make too much since you can store surplus in an airtight container.

2 Mix the two materials, using a pliable knife or palette knife, until they are completely blended and no streaks remain. It is easier to mix them in a small dish.

TOOLS & MATERIALS

Bronze Powder

Clear wax

Proprietary metallic wax

Palette knife for mixing

Cotton cloth for buffing

Stencil and stencil brush

Masking tape for making lines

Applying Metallic Wax

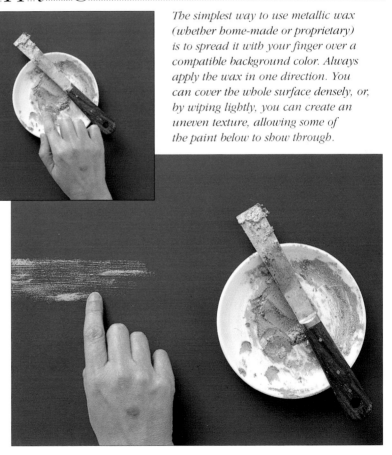

The simplest way to use metallic wax (whether home-made or proprietary) is to spread it with your finger over a compatible background color. Always apply the wax in one direction. You can cover the whole surface densely, or, by wiping lightly, you can create an uneven texture, allowing some of the paint below to show through.

Making Lines

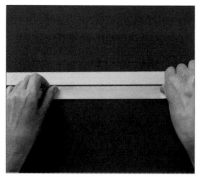

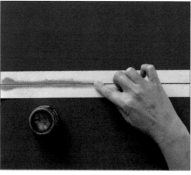

1 Pencil a guideline for position.
Place masking tape along the line.
Place a second piece about ⅛in/3mm
below. It is easiest to handle short
pieces of tape, up to 1½ft/46cm.

2 Press the edges of the tape well to
prevent wax from seeping underneath. With your finger (or a stencil
brush) wipe a very small amount of
metallic wax along the gap.

3 Remove the masking tape when
the work is finished. Allow to dry
overnight, then buff to a sheen with a
soft cotton cloth.

Using Stencils

1 Take a little metallic wax on a
stencil brush. Wipe any excess
wax onto the stencil frame, leaving
only a very small amount on the end
of the brush.

2 Brush lightly with a sweeping
motion over the stencil to leave
a thin layer of metallic wax. Allow
to dry overnight, then buff with
a soft cloth.

PITFALLS
If the wax is applied too thickly,
it may seep underneath the
stencil or create a ridge of wax.
If this occurs, leave the wax to
dry overnight. Then, using a
small knife, scrape away the
excess wax before buffing
the work.

Stenciled Lampshade
ABOVE *An unpainted parchment
lampshade was stenciled at random
with dark gold metallic wax and a
little copper metallic wax. The
finished lampshade was left unvarnished. When the light is turned on,
the stencils form silhouettes.*

Waxed Gold Frame

LEFT This ornate frame was bought with a plain blue-stained wooden finish. It has been enhanced with a light touch of metallic wax to highlight the tips of the carving. Two tones of wax, a warm reddish-gold and a light yellowish-gold, were used to give it life.

COLOR COMBINATIONS

Greenish-gold on pale yellow-ocher

Silver on pure white

Greenish-gold on terra-cotta

Reddish-gold on gray

Stenciled Mirror

RIGHT AND BELOW A wooden dressing-table mirror painted a rich, dark brown, was stenciled with a warm reddish-metallic wax, in imitation of a fabric design. The design repeats in a regular pattern around the edges and in a random way on the base of the mirror.

Waxed Birds Picture

LEFT A craft knife was used to etch this design on the surface, removing the gold metallic wax to reveal the dark base color underneath.

Verdigris

Verdigris Fruit Bowl

This bowl is made of wood with a metal rim. It was coated in a reddish-metallic wax, then covered with a brown shellac (garnet polish). Denatured alcohol/ methylated spirits mixed with pale blue-green paint was poured over the rim, and the bowl was tipped to make the mixture run down the side and onto the base.

W HEN EXPOSED TO AIR, the surface of copper develops bluish-green deposits over time, called verdigris, which can vary in color from pale to quite dark. To achieve this effect, start by rubbing a base of copper-colored metallic wax onto the surface of your item, then coat it with shellac (see pp. 14–15). You can then pour or puddle a mixture of denatured alcohol/methylated spirits and water-base green paint over the surface. Although the paint has a water base and the alcohol has a spirit base, they will just cohere if mixed thinly, with more alcohol than paint. The mixture leaves deposits of green paint on the surface of the shellac. Because the alcohol is the solvent for shellac, it also leaves streaks. The result is a beautiful combination of the warm, shiny copper and the cooler, flat green. To retain the contrast, do not apply varnish.

VERDIGRIS IN CLOSE-UP

To redistribute areas of green paint on an object you have already covered, creating a build-up of green in some areas and clearer patches in others, pour denatured alcohol/methylated spirits alone over the object. Tip the object to control the direction of the flow.

TOOLS & MATERIALS

Copper or reddish-metallic wax

Brush for applying denatured alcohol/-methylated spirits and paint mixture

Bluish-green water-base paint

Denatured alcohol/ methylated spirits

Shellac and brush for applying it

The Basic Technique

1 *Any color base will work for this technique, because the copper or reddish metallic wax completely covers the base. Use your finger or a stencil brush to spread the wax on.*

2 *Cover the wax with a coat of shellac (see pp. 14–15), using a soft brush. The type of shellac you use (here garnet polish) depends on the depth of color you want.*

3 *Mix three parts denatured alcohol/ methylated spirits to one part blue-green water-base flat paint. Tilt the waxed item, then press a loaded brush at its top to make the liquid run down (above). Apply more paint or more denatured alcohol/methylated spirits in places where you want either a build-up of paint or a clearer area (right).*

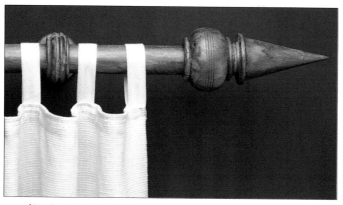

Verdigris Curtain Pole

ABOVE *Copper wax was rubbed all over this wooden curtain pole and finial, which were then coated in clear shellac. Two bluish-green paints were then mixed separately with denatured alcohol/methylated spirits and poured randomly over the pole, to make it resemble verdigrised copper.*

ALTERNATIVE

Instead of using copper wax, you can use copper metal leaf. The method remains the same after the metal is applied (see *The Basic Technique* on p. 85). Here the paint and alcohol mixture was dabbed on with a brush rather than streaked.

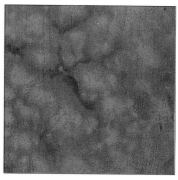

Highlighted Corbel

ABOVE *This plaster corbel has been prepared with reddish-gold copper wax and brown shellac (garnet polish). Pale and dark green paints mixed separately with denatured alcohol/methylated spirits were then dribbled over the front. Some areas, like the eyes and mouth, were highlighted with spots of paint mixture.*

Weather-beaten Frame

ABOVE *The weather-beaten effect was created using bright and pale green paint mixed with denatured alcohol/methylated spirits, over a copper wax and garnet polish. The warmer copper effect occured where the shellac had built up (bottom).*

Verdigris Lantern

RIGHT This zinc lantern needed no special preparation. It was rubbed all over with copper wax, then coated with light shellac. The paint and denatured alcohol/methylated spirits mixture was poured from above and was allowed to build up in certain places to make a variegated verdigris effect.

Copper Baseboard

BELOW Copper metal leaf was covered with garnet polish to make this unusual baseboard. A pale paint mixture was dribbled down it in irregular patches. Some areas were wiped so that more of the copper leaf could be seen.

COLOR COMBINATIONS

Clear shellac and light blue-green on pale greenish-gold

Brown shellac (garnet polish) and bright green on gold

Dark shellac (button polish) and middle blue-green on dark gold

Brown shellac (garnet polish) and middle blue-green on copper

PITFALLS

If you use too much paint it can become thick and crusted at the top of your work, as shown in this example. Here the color is also too garish and bright. Although the result is fun, it does not really resemble verdigris.

Combining Techniques

YOU CAN EASILY COMBINE two or more of the techniques in this book on one piece of furniture. Some combinations are less effective than others – when combining real gold leaf with metallic paint, for example, the paint dulls over time, while the gold continues to sparkle. Choose those techniques that are most suitable to your objects and that you can tackle easily. A few ideas are shown here, but there are many other possible combinations.

You can also apply many of the techniques demonstrated on metal leaf to bronze powders. Experiment with the techniques, mixing and matching to come up with your own combinations.

Highlighting Raised Surfaces (pp. 46–49)

Using Chemicals (pp. 62–67)

Distressing (pp. 58–61)

Distressed Leaf Motif

ABOVE *Dutch metal leaf was laid over terra-cotta paint, then exposed to fumes from a mixture of 4 parts potassium sulfide to 1 part ammonium sulfate. It was painted dark green and wiped off, then the metal leaf was removed over the "grapes" to reveal the base.*

Hand-painted, Bronze-powdered Block

RIGHT *Leaves of yellow ocher were painted in water-base paint over a transfer Dutch metal base. The central stems were delineated with a line of water-base size covered with bronze powder.*

Hand Painting on Metal Leaf (pp. 34–37)

Bronze Powders (pp. 72–75)

Highlighting Raised Surfaces (pp. 46–49)

Distressing (pp. 58–61)

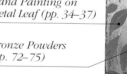

Bronze Powders (pp. 72–75)

Incising (pp. 54–57)

Decorated Headboard

LEFT *The shell-like motif was highlighted using brown paint. The panel below it and the center of the two main panels were incised through brown paint to reveal the Dutch metal leaf. The central bar was distressed with mineral spirit/ turpentine, and bronze powders were used to decorate the outer border of the central panels.*

Spirit-dyed and Distressed Table

LEFT AND BELOW The greenish-blue base was covered with loose and transfer metal leaf. The top was painted with neat spirit dyes, diluted in places with denatured alcohol/methylated spirits and then protected with an oil-base varnish. The sides and leg were waxed with steelwool, in places, revealing the base color.

Distressing
(pp. 58–61)

Distressing
(pp. 58–61)

Spirit Dyes
(pp. 50–53)

Using
Chemicals
(pp. 62–67)

Hand
Painting on
Metal Leaf
(pp. 34–37)

Distressed and Hand-painted Candlestick

ABOVE The terra-cotta base was covered in Dutch metal leaf and marked with copper nitrate in stripes and dots. Green paint was then used to encircle the spots and emphasize the lines. In some places the metal leaf was scratched back to reveal the terra-cotta base.

Distressed and Stenciled Door Panels

ABOVE These panels were covered in aluminum leaf and distressed with wax to reveal the gray-blue paint underneath. They were then varnished with a coat of pale shellac and stenciled with a 1930's-style pattern using a solid blue water-base paint.

Distressing
(pp. 58–61)

Hand Painting on
Metal Leaf (pp. 34–37)
with a stencil

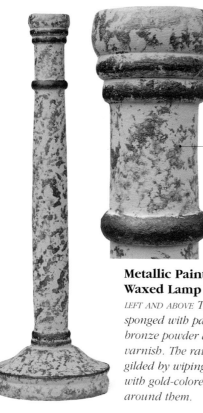

Metallic Wax (pp. 80–83)

Metallic Paints (pp. 76–79)

Metallic Paint and Waxed Lamp Base

LEFT AND ABOVE The base was sponged with paint made from bronze powder and water-base varnish. The raised rings were gilded by wiping a brush coated with gold-colored metallic wax around them.

Metallic Paint and Crackle-glazed Panel

BELOW This panel was gilded with transfer aluminum leaf to give it the look of an old mirror. A metallic paint made with medium gold bronze powders in water-base varnish, was painted around the sides over a crackle glaze medium. This produced large, pronounced cracks.

Transfer Metal Leaf (pp. 26–29)

Metallic paints (pp. 76–79) over a crackle glaze medium

Hand Painting on Metal Leaf (pp. 34–37)

Distressing (pp. 58–61)

Spirit Dyes (pp. 50–53)

Bronze Powders (pp. 72–75)

Bronze-powdered Frame and Distressed Frame

FAR LEFT The greenish-gray base was covered with water-base size and medium gold bronze powder. The carved area was gently rubbed revealing the green. On the inner area and top molding, a coat of brown spirit dyes was dabbed with denatured alcohol/methylated spirits. *LEFT* The blue base was covered in loose copper leaf and rubbed softly with white spirit and medium steel-wool. Brown paint was lightly brushed over, partially covering the surface.

Waxed and Bronze Powdered Storage Tin

LEFT AND FAR LEFT These old storage tins were painted with black metal paint. The designs for the bands and central area were made with stencils and gold-colored metallic wax, then coated in shellac. Finally, light gold-colored bronze powder was applied over water-base size to highlight the raised edges and parts of the design.

Bronze Powders (pp. 72–75)

Metallic Wax (pp. 80–83)

Metallic Wax (pp. 80–83)

Bronze Powders (pp. 72–75)

Loose Metal Leaf (pp. 22–25)

Metallic Paints (pp. 76–79)

Metallic Paint and Metal Leaf Wastepaper Basket

ABOVE Plastic bubblewrap painted with gold-colored metallic paint was pressed against the side of this green-painted wastepaper basket to create a unique design. Copper leaf was placed in an abstract pattern round the top and in strips.

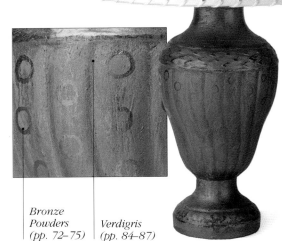

Bronze Powders (pp. 72–75)

Verdigris (pp. 84–87)

Verdigrised and Bronze-powdered Lamp Base

LEFT This china lamp base was verdigrised with a reddish-gold and medium green paint, then varnished with shellac. Circles of oil-base size were then painted around the sides and covered with bright crimson and reddish-copper bronze powders.

Index

How to Find Supplies

The tools and materials you need for the techniques demonstrated in this book are generally available from speciality art supply and paint stores. To find a store near you, try looking in your local telephone directory under paint, art, craft supplies, decorative materials, or even gilding. If you are on the Internet, you can look there under the same categories, or you can try speciality magazines on crafts and interior decoration, where many of the stores and suppliers place advertisements. If there are no stores in your neighborhood, don't despair as many of them have mail order facilities and you can send for a catalogue.

You can also visit Annie Sloan's Internet site – *www.anniesloan.co.uk* – for more information.

Acknowledgments

This book could not have been produced without the tremendous assistance of the Home Team – David, Henry, Felix, and Hugo – and the Away Team – the photographer, Geoff Dann, his assistant, Gavin Durrant, and the designer, Steve Wooster. Many thanks also to Colin Ziegler, Claire Waite, and Mandy Greenfield for their patience and understanding.

I am also very grateful to Stuart Stevenson for advice on gilding products and many aspects of the gilding process (Stuart R Stevenson, Artists and Gilding Materials, 68 Clerkenwell Road, London EC1M 5QA) and to Carolyn Koch de Gooreynd, Kate Pollard, David, Henry, and Felix Manuel for their help in the studio, and to Hugo Manuel for his support.

All the gilding products used in this book are available from Relics of Witney, but I would like to thank the following for providing other materials: The Bradley Collection for the curtain poles on pages 72 and 87 (The Bradley Collection, The Granary, Flowton Brook, Flowton, Suffolk IP8 4LJ); Bennison Fabrics for the material covering the chair seat on page 22 (Bennison Fabrics, Holbein Place, London SW1W 8NL); Finesse of Oxford for all the decorative plasterwork (Finesse Ltd. Unit 5, 7 Westway, Botley Oxford); Ton Goossens and Hans Schut in The Netherlands for the plaque on pages 48–49; Tanja van Sijp for the plaques on page 87; G and A Broom of Macclesfield for the hand-painted plant container on page 37 and wastepaper basket on page 66 (G & A Broom Unit 6, Clarence Mill, Bollington, Macclesfield, Cheshire SK10 5JT); and Truro Designs for the Dutch metal candle holder on page 67.

Thanks also to Lewis Ward of Whistler Brushes, whose speciality brushes feature often throughout the book (Lewis Ward and Co., 128 Fortune Green Road, London, NW6) and all those at Relics of Witney, especially Bret Wiles, Chris Walker, and Ray Russell.